THE PHOENIX LEADERSHIP PROGRAMME

The Pheonix Leadership Programme

Book and Cover design by Derek Murphy

ISBN-13: 978-1491274064 (Paperback)

10 9 8 7 6 5 4 3 2 1

THE PHOENIX LEADERSHIP PROGRAMME

MAKE YOUR BEST, BETTER

JOHN BABB

To my wife Uzma

Without whom this book would not have been possible.

CONTENTS

THE PHOENIX LEADERSHIP PROGRAMME (PLP)

Introduction: What is it? And what can you learn from it?

The Phoenix Leadership Programme (PLP) is a strategic yet practical approach to effective leadership. This book can be used as a stand-alone method of learning about and applying the Phoenix Leadership Programme. Alternatively it can be used in conjunction with the Phoenix Leadership Mentoring Programme, delivered exclusively by the author and his associates (see the training and development page at: www.experiencemyculture.com for further information).

By stripping away overcomplicated approaches that you may have experienced in the past, the PLP offers a straightforward strategy; one that serves to identify the key elements of effective leadership, the foundation of which is based on the 'Leadership Cycle': Knowledge, Understanding, Skills, Application and Results (K.U.S.A.R.) fig 1.1. This five-stage model identifies how real development and effectiveness is achieved, reviewed and maintained.

The PLP challenges the traditional and often rigid thinking regarding the separate and distinct roles of management and leadership, suggesting that there should be conscious and intelligent interplay between these two functions through the use of a 'Leadership Continuum' (fig 1.2).

This book guides the reader through the process required to appreciate, understand and apply the principles of the Phoenix Leadership Programme. It is essential reading for anyone aspiring to become a truly effective leader.

The book reviews fundamental components such as:

- Identifying outcomes (personal, strategic and organisational).
- Values and how to reinforce them.
- Effective communication.
- Six principles of effective leadership
- Communicating your vision to others
- Developing cohesiveness within teams.
- Creating buy-in.
- Managing and resolving conflict.
- Learning from the past.

- Increasing self-awareness.
- Creating the 'mood for development'.
- The PLP 'Boomerang Theory' of Leadership.
- Options and Consequences (Case Study One: Appendix 'A')

These are in essence, the core elements of the Phoenix Leadership Programme.

The Phoenix Leadership Programme

Some sources, for example: Herman Cain, former C.E.O of Godfather's Pizza and Roger V. Fulton (author), suggest that leadership is a matter of common sense. In contrast, 'Great Man' and 'Trait' theories of leadership advocate that leaders are born and not made. In other words 'you either have it or you don't'. A third school of thought maintains that the application of sound leadership theory is absolutely vital for anyone seeking to be a successful leader.

The Phoenix Leadership Programme bridges the gap between the theoretical and the practical, promoting effective leadership through the Leadership Cycle: Knowledge, Understanding, Skills, Application and Results (K.U.S.A.R. fig 1.1).

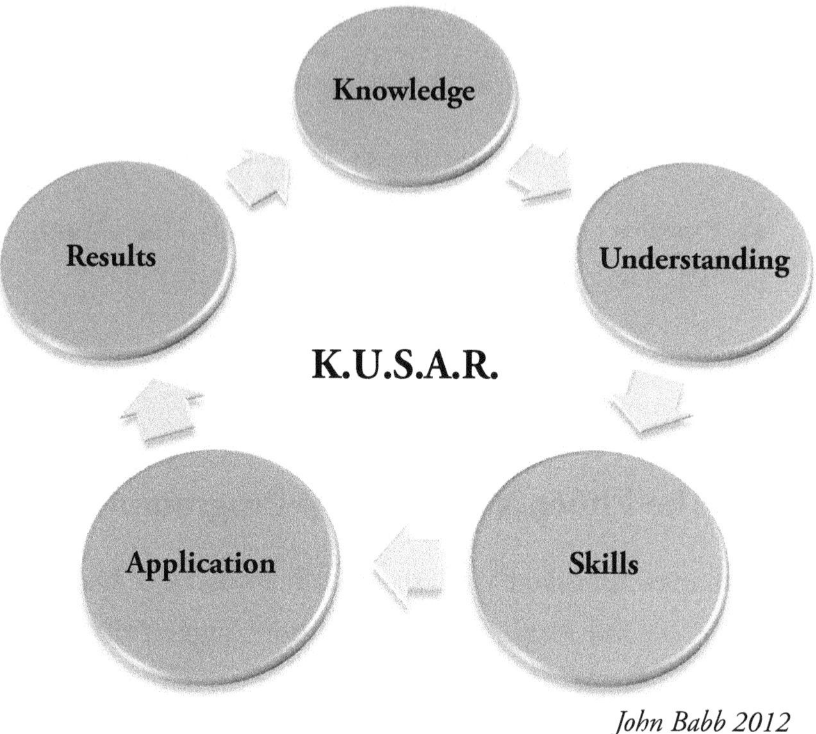

Figure 1.1: The Leadership Cycle—Knowledge, Understanding, Skills, Application & Results (K.U.S.A.R.)

Knowledge: having an appreciation or awareness of a theory through training, practice or experience.

Understanding: the perception of the significance or cause of something.

Skills: possessing the ability to apply oneself well, whether through natural or acquired abilities.

Application: the action of putting something into operation/ practice.

Results: the consequence or outcome of your decisions or actions.

Leadership

Traditional thinking, such as that associated with Peter F. Drucker and Stephen Covey, suggests that there is a significant difference between leadership and management. Managers are seen as being responsible for directing people and resources, ensuring that they move in an agreed direction according to organisational instruction and values, while leaders set the strategic direction of a group or organisation. They establish direction based on organisational values.

The Phoenix Leadership Programme suggests that, at various stages of the leadership continuum (fig 1.2), there are shifts between the roles of leadership and management; the interplay between the two roles being a significant and acceptable factor in the successful development and application of effective leadership. In fact, the Phoenix Leadership Programme maintains that continued conscious interplay between the two roles, to a greater or lesser degree, is a necessity, and as you move towards your desired outcome, personal and or staff development, it may assist in the achievement of reflective competence in action (fig 1.3).

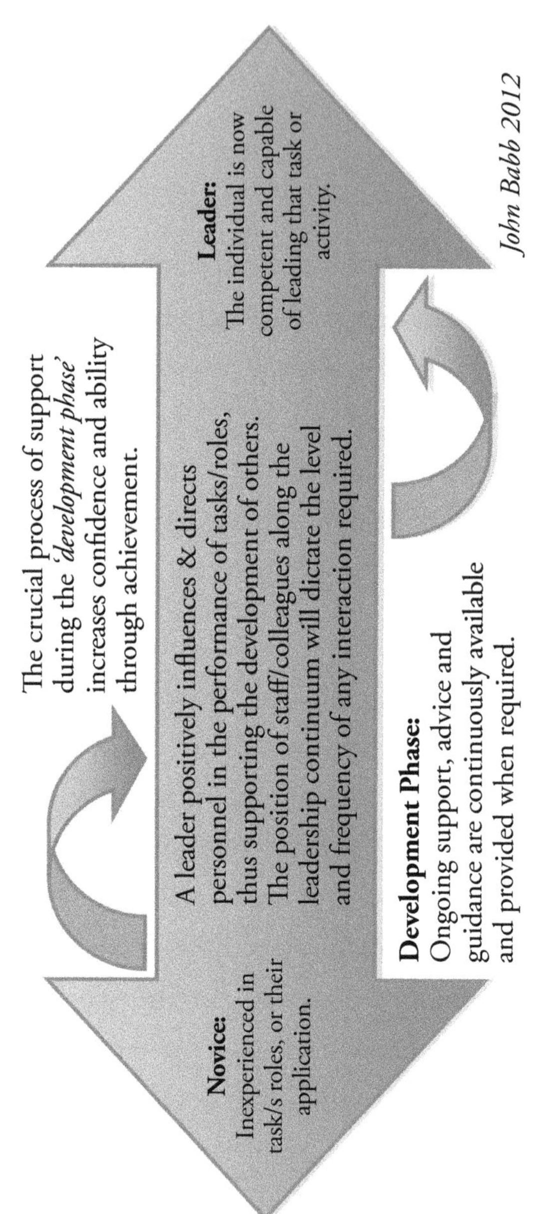

Figure 1.2: The Leadership Continuum—This model identifies the process whereby individuals are provided with the opportunity to develop into leaders in their own roles

(creating a foundation upon which they can add greater levels of leadership responsibility), creating: buy-in, staff and organisational development as well as reinforcing the five-stage leadership cycle (K.U.S.A.R.).

The Phoenix Leadership Programme also builds on the view that the strategic direction of an organisation should be based on its values (principles, standards and ethics) that are: visible, easily understood and implemented throughout the organisation. The effective communication of these values ensures that your staff and colleagues understand that they underpin the application of the organisational skills and that these skills underpin their values. The author suggests that where this is understood, your people are less likely to engage in risky, questionable or illegal practices.

Who should use the Phoenix Leadership Programme?

The programme has been developed for anyone who wants to be a thinker, communicator, supervisor, manager and or leader. Using the Phoenix approach an effective leader will become all of these and much more. The Phoenix Leadership Programme is unique in that it simultaneously supports a top down and bottom up approach to leadership and development, identified by the Reflective Competence in Action concept: An approach that enables the user to monitor the awareness and capabilities of themselves and others, and apply or manage that awareness/capability in theory and or in practice, through fluid and competent reflection (fig 1.3).

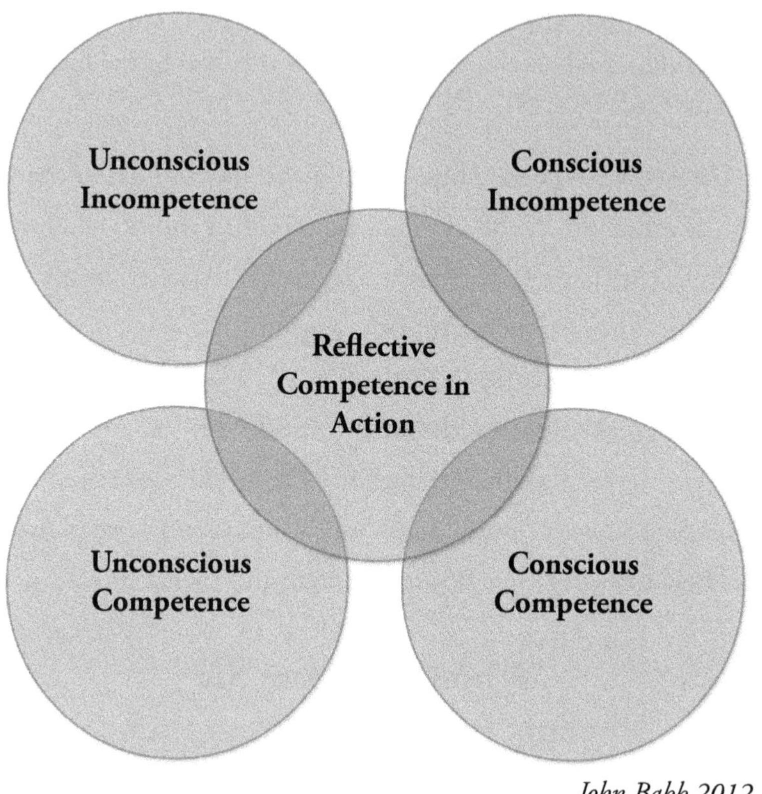

John Babb 2012

Figure 1.3: Reflective Competence in Action—An approach that enables the user to monitor the awareness and capabilities of themselves and others, and apply or manage that awareness/capability in theory and or in practice, through fluid and competent reflection.

The Phoenix approach is universal. The six Leadership Principles outlined can be applied in whole or in part across all organisations, from small community projects to multi-national corporations.

INTRODUCTION

Like you, the author wants your organisation to be inclusive and productive, supporting the development of its people to achieve your goals.

The use of the Phoenix Leadership Programme has the distinct advantage of preparing individuals, teams and organisations for progression and succession planning. Each organisation that utilises the Phoenix Leadership Programme and its principles of leadership recognises the need to continuously formulate outcomes and to constantly reassess those outcomes in line with the values of the organisation (thus reinforcing those values, and making them second nature) and will benefit from the organisation being uniquely placed to identify individuals who have been the subject of a well thought-out, consistent and comprehensive development programme. This makes succession planning a reality, as opposed to identifying one person as the successor for a key position prior to its incumbent leaving the job. The Phoenix Leadership Programme enables you to identify and develop a number of highly skilled individuals, putting the organisation in the enviable position of being able to choose from the best rather than having only one option to fill the post.

As an individual undertaking Phoenix Leadership Programme, you will experience a level of personal and professional development that eludes many of your peers and will serve to identify you as an effective leader, opening more doors for your continued personal and professional progression.

THE IMPORTANCE AND APPLICATION OF LEADERSHIP

Remember the Leadership Cycle: K.U.S.A.R.?

How often have you attended a leadership course and at the end of it walked away with more confidence in your ability, full of ideas and theories about leadership, only to have that confidence and new found knowledge slip away from you as the hours, days and weeks pass?

Well, you're not the only one. Some delegates who have attended leadership courses agree to hold regular meetings with their co-attendees; meetings that allow them to discuss the techniques learned on the course, the opportunities they have had to use those techniques and what challenges, if any, they have faced and successfully overcome as a result. Some of those groups do quite well and last for several weeks or months after the course has ended, you may even make some really good contacts that last for some time into the future, people with whom you can share information with, bounce ideas off etc.

For some people this is useful but not quite enough because they continue to want more information, a better steer on how to lead their staff/colleagues effectively, along with practical, day-to-day techniques that can assist them in becoming a more competent and effective leader.

The feelings and concerns that you may be having are quite normal. If you weren't concerned about your performance and the impact you have on the people around you, you would probably be an ineffective leader. Seeking feedback, advice and guidance on your leadership style is very productive; it helps to maintain focus, allows you to consider different options which may help you to improve and can provide you with an objective point of view.

Communication

The leader needs to have the ability to communicate at all levels and see the bigger picture, something that you will have all heard at one time or another, but what does it all mean?

It means that as a leader you must be able to step away from the question, task or problem at hand and assess how any course of action you choose to undertake will affect the overall outcome. Where possible, the decision/s based on this simple principle should be communicated to your team/s. However, where this is not possible or appropriate, you should have developed or be in the process of developing an understanding within the group that there is good reason for not explaining the decision at that time, highlighting that, when appropriate, the reason behind the decision will be explained. Your team doesn't want to feel excluded, so keep them informed whenever possible, it will make them feel valued.

Being able to communicate with people at all levels means that you should be able to express your point of view effectively to anyone, whether they are a junior, the same or a more senior rank or grade to yourself. More often than not you will know someone who can speak passionately about a teacher, lecturer or mentor, someone who struck a chord with them, someone who always made things make sense, even the most complicated topics.

As a leader it is your job to find the best way of communicating with your team, regarding them firstly as individuals with their own wants and needs, and secondly as members of the organisation with specific roles and or responsibilities. Being able to achieve this means that you appreciate what their primary motivations are, which in itself will assist you to communicate what it is you are attempting to achieve in line with any shared values your staff/colleagues have with the organisation. This will go a long way to making them feel like part of a team, one they have something in common with. Informing your team of what it is you require of them promotes a greater level of understanding, reduces confusion and assists/allows them to identify their own strengths and weaknesses. This can also provide the opportunity for them to ask for any support, advice or guidance they may require, conversely offering themselves up (if they posses a high level of competence in a particular area) as support for anyone else that may require it. This is how you start to actively build a group/team that works well.

In essence, communication is about breaking things down to their lowest common denominator, rephrasing and then presenting them in a way that promotes a more complete understanding of a message or the task at hand. An effective leader appreciates how difficult a task this is. S/he stimulates those around them by providing clarity in instruction along with an ability to translate detailed and complicated information from both internal and external sources. People gravitate towards such leaders because they provide information in a format they can understand and present it in a way that makes them feel worthwhile.

THE SIX PRINCIPLES OF EFFECTIVE LEADERSHIP

1- Inform, 2- Lead, 3- Discuss

The Phoenix Leadership Programme identifies six principles of effective leadership. The first three are: Inform, Lead and Discuss and the final three (which you will find under decision making) are: Listen, Consider and Act.

Inform

If you take over a new team/section, you should inform your personnel who you are and apprise them of your background, including any relevant experience or qualifications. It is important to inform your colleagues of your vision for the future, what you expect from them as individuals and as a team, identify the values that underpin what it is you will be doing and how you envisage that you/they will achieve it. It may be prudent to inform them of what the organisation requires of you as a leader as well as what they (your team) can expect from you.

Why inform?

This approach will provide your new colleagues with a wealth of information, not only about who you are, obviously, but also about your expectations thus answering questions that many people will be asking themselves and each other. You also present yourself as a confident leader, one who is there to get the job done; a leader who has the ability to hold their attention and is focused on the immediacy of the task at hand. The fact that you have shared your vision with your team means that you have a plan, a plan that has the organisational values at its core. This generates the very real perception that your plan is achievable, even at such an early stage.

Lead

You are likely to encounter some members of your team who are happy to accept your (new) vision and are ready to hit the ground running. They will be led by your example, demonstrate your ability to lead by doing just that, be the person who is first in and the last out. Show that you are someone who actively promotes the values of the organisation and their vision for the organisation through what they say and what they do on a day-to-day basis, it will encourage your team to do the same. You may find that some of your colleagues are not fully committed to your vision at first and will wait on the sidelines performing their duties as requested, though not yet convinced of your approach. You are also likely to encounter those who are less enthusiastic and will take every opportunity to question your judgment and your vision, both in public and or in private. It is at times such as these that your ability to ***discuss*** opposing issues or concerns with the relevant member(s) of your team is very important. Effective leaders are keen to discuss issues that arise, making it their business to ensure that their vision is clear and their message is understood. An unwillingness or inability to do this can lead to a breakdown in communication, which in turn may lead to a loss of respect for that leader, the knock-on effect being that when a team loses faith in you, you will likely lose faith in and respect for them and their collective ability as a team.

Flexibility is the key. Be careful not to bow to the will of the team, continuously answering questions in an attempt to defend what it is you are trying to achieve. That is not leadership. There are times to answer questions about what you intend to do and how you intend to do it. Equally, it is sometimes appropriate to inform those concerned that the time for discussion has come to an end and it is time for them to take action in order to realise your vision and that of the organisation. You have already demonstrated the fact that you are a reasoned, considered and intelligent leader, this may now be the time to demonstrate that you have the ability to take definitive action in order to get the job done. Such an assertive approach is usually only implemented when all other attempts at diplomacy have either broken down or, in certain circumstances, are deemed inappropriate due to time constraints or other considerations. As the leader you will need to decide if and when an explanation for such an approach is warranted.

You should make it your business to know exactly what the organisation requires of you as a leader. This provides you with the ability to establish your desired outcome in line with organisational values and expectations. The use of signposts and achievable objectives will assist you in arriving at your designated outcome, as well as providing you with a more stable platform from which to communicate what you require from your team, both as individuals and as a collective, make them aware of the values that underpin what you/they will be doing and how you (along with the roles they are assigned to undertake) intend to achieve it.

Decision Making/Problem Solving
(Leadership Principles 4, 5 & 6 are found here):
4- Listen, 5- Consider, 6- Act

Some leaders find the process of decision-making difficult or uncomfortable; they mull over documents, policies, and procedures before deciding upon a course of action. This process is time consuming, costly and rather one-dimensional, in so much as it applies the thought process of one person. As experienced as this person may be, the process simply fails to consider the collective knowledge, skills, experience and abilities of the people who work with or for them.

If you have had the foresight to develop, or are currently developing, a team (as discussed in: 'Developing a sense of team') that you can trust, you should know and appreciate the fact that you have allowed, assisted and or enabled them to develop a range of valuable skills and experiences in and around your area of business, whether in general or specific terms. With that in mind you should appreciate that you have access to a valuable collective and diverse resource: your colleagues. The time and effort that you have spent on their development starts to pay off. You have not only made them feel like a part of something bigger than themselves, you have communicated that they have a positive contribution to make to you, the team and the organisation. This is a perspective that you can reinforce by undertaking a simple yet under used activity: asking for their thoughts/observations, opinions and suggestions.

When faced with a dilemma or difficult situation/decision there is nothing wrong with seeking the best advice available. For some, this is the time to call in expensive consultants who offer generic or specific advice on a range of issues and topics.

The alternative is to seek out those amongst your group, team and or organisation who possess the specific knowledge, skills and abilities required to address the prevailing issues/s, have a meeting with them, analyse the problem, dilemma or task at hand and ask them how best to proceed. Your job is to present the issue to the group and identify your desired outcome. This involves employing principles four, five and six of the Phoenix Leadership Programme: Listen, Consider and Act.

Listen to what your group of experts are telling you about the issue at hand, encourage them to be as open as possible about how to achieve either your personal or the organisational outcome, (they may be one in the same thing), as well as identifying any potential pitfalls and associated considerations that may arise.

Consider everything they are telling you. Even if you don't like what you are hearing, you may not be in possession of all of the facts or up-to-date research relating to the issue, where as they might. If you have additional information your team should know about, share it with them, where operational procedure allows; this will assist them in arriving at a more appropriate solution.

Act - The decision you make should be based on all of the available information coupled with the advice and guidance of your subject experts (your team/s). Their input is extremely valuable and should play a pivotal part in your decision making process. It is essential to apprise them of the decision you have made at the earliest opportunity. Be mindful of the fact that the decision you make is your responsibility and rests with you.

This approach can be applied by effective leaders everywhere. There are reasons that you spend so much time and money on staff development; a failure to utilise their expertise in a productive manner can lead staff/colleagues to question the value of their role, as well as considering whether or not there are greater rewards and personal fulfillment to be had elsewhere.

Critical Thinking

A definition of critical thinking is: a process or method of thinking that enables an individual to question assumptions.

The ability to apply critical thinking is an essential part of effective leadership. Being able to consider and process information in a way that considers a number of different variables and outcomes, allows you to make competent and effective decisions based on all of the information available at that time. By definition, being a critical thinker means that you do not take things for granted. Certain things that may seem obvious or common sense are not always as they appear and, as a result, can become the source of costly mistakes and misunderstandings. Effective leaders don't leave such things to chance, they ask questions, check and double-check, ensuring that they have considered the most reasoned and logical solution to the situation that presents itself. They assess the level of understanding amongst their team and proceed, while being open to ideas and suggestions from their team along the way, knowing that they need to remain flexible enough to alter their approach if the situation demands it.

Listening

Many leaders claim to be good listeners, but what is listening?

Listening is an active process that allows you to demonstrate that you are receiving and understanding the information people are sharing with you. Active Listening is a skill that involves nodding appropriately, paraphrasing, summarising, the use of attentive spoken cues such as, aha, yeah, ah, mm, etc. This technique also communicates your interest in the person or persons with whom you are communicating. In general, active listening allows people to feel more engaged in the conversation, which results in them being more inclined to share information with you, primarily because you appear to be genuinely interested in what they have to say and also because (through this process) you are demonstrating your respect for them. In contrast, passive listening is the exact opposite and is less likely to make people want to engage with you. Interaction becomes a chore; people will often disengage and or simply walk away.

COMMUNICATING YOUR VISION

It is not unusual for a leader to have vision, a concept of what he or she wishes to achieve, along with how they intend to make it happen. A vision can be the result of an epiphany, a well worked idea or a thought sparked by a friend or colleague, whether connected with the project or not. The question is how do you communicate your vision to your team?

Are you a leader who takes time to share the vision or are you so involved with the task at hand that you either forget to mention where you are heading or become so wrapped up in the things going on around you that you are under the impression that you have already informed your team what it is you want them to do and how you would like them to do it? The latter is quite a common occurrence. It creates confusion, frustration and conflict between leaders, their teams and individual members of that team. Because people expect their counterparts to be up-to-speed with their ideas, they believe that other people have already been apprised of the vision, have answers to questions they think have already been asked and have completed tasks they think that people have been given.

In such cases leaders can often be accused of being absent-minded, preoccupied or simply ineffective. Either way, this situation is avoidable. As a leader it is up to you to, not only have the vision, but also to communicate that vision effectively. You need to ensure, wherever possible, either personally or through your supervisory/managerial staff, that every member of your team has a good working knowledge and understanding of what it is you are attempting to achieve. And how you, with their help, are seeking to achieve that vision. Where there are changes to what has already been shared and or agreed, take it upon yourself to identify those changes and communicate them effectively to the people who need to know. This level of communication is a basic necessity, one that helps to avoid misunderstandings that can plague tasks and projects alike, regardless of their scale and relative importance.

DEVELOPING A SENSE OF TEAM

This is one of the most difficult things to achieve. A sense of team can only be achieved if you demonstrate that you regard your people as being worthy and capable of working alongside you and each other, and thus possessing the ability to deliver your vision.

Value their contributions; if people feel that their contributions are either ignored or simply not taken seriously, they are much less likely to continue sharing. This is where we start to lose the person and the team suffers as a result.

Share your knowledge with them and encourage them to share their knowledge with you and other members of the team in an open forum, team meetings and when working side-by-side. Share findings, ideas and discoveries. A failure to share in this way causes people to think that you are involved in a project purely for personal gain, your team will follow your lead and eventually, you will have a group of people more interested in their own personal advancement, with little or no investment in the team, its development or its survival.

Take care to demonstrate that you regard your team members equally and without favoritism. Favoritism is a sure fire way to create infighting, rumours and resentment, none of which are productive, all of which will cause arguments and dissent, which will only serve to weaken your team.

Be open to new ways of working. It is sometimes the case that one or more members of your team will identify a new or alterative way of working, so be open to suggestions and where possible consider trials. If you have solicited input, be mindful not to dismiss it out of hand, if something cannot be done! It is prudent to be in a position to explain why it should not be attempted.

Take overall responsibility for errors within your team but share the glory of success. Taking responsibility for your team in this way demonstrates that you regard yourself as an integral part of that team and that you support and value the team as a whole. The willingness to share success with your team reinforces this belief, further cementing your role as leader.

Do not allow weaknesses, mistakes and fear to hold the team back. Expose everyone to training, development and advancement. Strengthen your/their weaknesses and make your best better.

The saying 'a chain is only as strong as its weakest link' is true enough. If you have a weaker member of your team, invest time, money (where appropriate) and effort into bringing their skills up to speed. This demonstrates a willingness to support individual team members for the good of the team and the organisation. Leaving them out of projects and placing them on the sidelines serves only to de-skill and de-motivate them. If a team member no longer has the desire or ability to continue within the team, discuss the situation with them, determine what obstacles may exist and work to remove them and formulate a tangible action plan which is workable for both parties. If you have tried this approach without success, consider letting them go, it may be time for both parties to move on. If this is the most productive course of action, where possible, provide them with the assistance they need to start again somewhere else. Any loss will have some impact on a team and how you are seen to manage this loss/transition will provide your team with valuable information about how you deal with people. In essence, this will come down to you being either good: considerate, caring, fair and supportive, or bad: dismissive, unhelpful, uncaring and cold. Leadership is not a popularity contest. That being said, 'Emotional Intelligence' (E.Q.) is an indicator of effective leadership and as such is not something that should be ignored. Peter Salovey and John D. Mayer coined the term Emotional Intelligence in 1990; it describes a form of intelligence (developed awareness) that allows an individual to monitor their own feelings and those of others.

CONFLICT RESOLUTION

Leaders all over the world understand that one of the many things they are expected to deal with is the management and or resolution of conflict. Conflict is common, it occurs on a day-to-day basis, between individuals, teams, supervisors, managers and leaders alike, many of whom have difficulty in pinpointing its cause as well as formulating a strategy (strategies) for dealing with it effectively. It is by no means insurmountable, and can be managed or resolved by establishing a flexible and acceptable outcome based on a number of manageable considerations.

The leader should consider the historical and factual components of any conflict, how it impacts upon them, their colleagues and ultimately the organisation, along with the possibility of managing or resolving the problem. The effective use of appropriate skills such as active listening, negotiation, non-verbal and verbal communication will assist in achieving your outcome. All of these component parts, when actively considered and skillfully implemented, will go a long way to managing or indeed resolving a situation before it becomes too problematic, i.e. when it begins to negatively affect the working relationships within your team and has a detrimental impact on your organisation's services. That being said, the techniques can be used to great effect following a breakdown in communication, however, in such circumstances it can be more difficult but not impossible to establish a workable outcome (see case study two; Appendix 'A').

One of the best ways of developing the skills required to manage and resolve conflict is by attending or buying-in a competent and practical conflict resolution course run by an experienced trainer/s; people who can make this, at times, difficult subject matter more understandable. A trainer that helps you to think and respond like an active participant, one who provides a detailed account of how values, psychology, physiology, negotiation and non-verbal communication can provide a key to the successful management and or resolution of conflict; a minimum requirement for an effective leader.

The Phoenix Conflict Resolution Training Programme is one such approach and is delivered exclusively by:

www.experiencemyculture.com

See their training and development page for further information.

CREATING BUY-IN

One of the most powerful ways of getting the most out of your team is to create buy-in (which is similar to, but in addition to, developing a sense of team), by getting your staff/colleagues to believe in the work that you and the organisation undertake.

Buy-in is about values: personal, professional and organisational. It may be possible to influence the likely success of this process at the recruitment stage by assessing the compatibility of your applicants' values and beliefs, through questioning and or the use of psychometric tests or other assessment tools (which is ultimately an organisational decision). However, the reality is that the majority of leaders will inherit pre-established teams, which is a more difficult proposition.

The Phoenix Leadership Programme identifies techniques which are applicable to newly formed and pre-established teams alike.

First and foremost, it is essential to know your desired outcome, as continually stated throughout this book. If you have no idea what you are trying to achieve, how will you know if you are on the right track or even if/when you have arrived at your goal? Equally important, how would you be able to get back on track if, for whatever reason/s, you become derailed? Once you have established your outcome, set about apprising your colleagues of your vision and provide a breakdown of how you intend to set about achieving it. This should include informing them of the part they are to play in this process, as well as asking them if they have any thoughts about your plans at this stage. There are times when your team may be very negative about the process you have identified and this could be due to a number of different reasons:

- Fear of the unknown.
- They may not have been listened to during a previous process of change and as a result be concerned that they may experience the same fate.
- Your staff/colleagues may have genuine concerns based on their experience and expertise in this field.

Whatever the circumstances of negativity, it is important for you to ask the team/s if they have any issues, listen to what they say and make an assessment of their concerns (consider) and act according to how you think the outcome will best be achieved. There may need to be a degree of flexibility regarding the outcome, timings may alter, objectives removed or others introduced. The decision on how best to proceed rests with you, but understand that this period of consultation is the beginning of your buy-in process. This means it is important that you demonstrate you have not only listened to what has been said, but also that you have considered it in light of all the available information. This may necessitate taking some time out to think about the teams' concerns and reporting back to them or, if you are comfortable in doing so, answering their questions in an open forum stating why you consider your plan to be the most productive way forward, providing sound evidence or examples that reinforce your point of view.

If you continue to experience a lack of support for the plan in question, it is up to you to draw a line in the sand, re-establish control and make a decision to either proceed or alter the plan. This will be dependent upon whether or not you are implementing a strict or rigid organisational directive or initiating a more flexible change programme. If it is an organisational directive (your hands are pretty much tied) there is nothing wrong with informing your colleagues of the fact that the decision to implement this model has been made at a level more senior than yours, but that you intend to do everything you can to make the process work, and work well.

Alternatively, one possible resolution is to you inform your staff/colleagues that you intend to undertake the process for a trial period, specifying the length of time, at the end of which you will assess the viability of the plan by measuring it against the set objectives. If things go well the plan remains in place. If however, there are issues relating to its long-term effectiveness, you will look at their concerns again alongside the additional evidence taken from the trial with a view to making changes.

You are effectively leading from the front by apprising your team of the decision that you have made and explaining why, as well as outlining the thought process that led to the decision itself. You are identifying, not only the process you employ in reaching those decisions, but also how you expect others to reach their decisions using the same or similar criteria, with the organisational values at the heart of their outcome based thinking and decision-making process. This can be further encouraged or reinforced, either actively or passively during your appraisal meetings or regular one-to-one sessions.

It is also important to appreciate that your colleagues will need your support in return. Encourage them to undertake training, to ask for advice/guidance and seek assistance from you and or other members of the team when they need it. This will help them to develop trust in you and in each other. Demonstrating such support promotes an increasingly capable and professional team, the team you want them to be. They will begin to share their ideas about how to make things better because you have instilled a sense of worth and commitment. They will want to promote the values you have identified because you consistently demonstrate reasons to believe in them.

Monitor this stage carefully, either personally or through your supervisor/s or manager/s, dependent upon how far along the leadership continuum they are (fig 1.2), and remember that you are there to challenge, support, advise and guide. If you encounter someone who is totally opposed to or incapable of change/development you should consider his or her position within your team, in line with the organisational values and the efficacy of the team.

LEARNING FROM THE PAST

Though it is not unusual for leaders to make reference to learning from the past, in practice this is rarely something that is given much consideration and more often than not relates to learning from the mistakes of the past. This is certainly one strategy. That being said, there is a much more productive way to learn from the past, allowing it to inform future practice and development in a way that promotes confidence in you, your abilities and your colleagues. If and when you find yourself in a position that you or those around you consider to be solid, good, productive or even outstanding, you need to be mindful of how and why you got there. Some will say that it isn't that important, what is important is that you have the kudos, accolades and the respect of your peers and the organisation. This may be true, in part, however, if you have little idea as to how and why this all happened, how can you hope to maintain your position? How can you maintain staff morale and avoid this success slipping through your fingers? The truth is, you cannot. Of course there is nothing to say that this will happen, but equally there is little to say that it will not.

Being willing to learn from the past helps you to shape, define and achieve your future outcome/s and associated objectives. The process can be as formal or as informal as you deem necessary, but there should be a process, one that you and your team follow closely. Taking time to assess why your processes worked well or why they worked less well and, at times, why they might not have worked at all, allows you to implement considered and productive changes.

What was the process in question? Did it follow policy? Is that practice or policy still fit for purpose? Who was responsible for implementing action/s? Was their background and or training consistent with what they were being asked to do?

If the answers to these or similar questions are "yes", and the process resulted in success, ask yourself if you could strengthen your position by either formalising the process or by having more people trained in this area, thereby boosting resilience. If however, the answers are negative, what is the outcome you are seeking to achieve? Is it personal, strategic or organisational (see: Creating the mood for development) or a combination thereof?

How do you propose to improve your own performance and that of your team? Being aware of your organisational values will assist you in answering these questions. This level of reflection and questioning may seem overwhelming at first, but in time, with practice, it becomes a useful, practical, consistent and an integral part of your continued progress and eventual success, allowing you to pinpoint what went well and why, or what went less well, or even wrong, and why. This will help you to make the necessary alterations, changes and developments required within you, your team/s, as well as your own individual or collective working practices.

SELF-AWARENESS

Developing an increased level of self-awareness, that is to say, an appreciation of how and why we respond to things and or people in the way that we do, can be assisted by the completion of psychometric tests, 360° feedback or some form of team roles assessment etc. Truly effective leadership necessitates that you acquire an increased level of self-awareness, as it will provide you with the skill to assess how you relate to people and in turn how they respond to you. This is one of the reasons why the most effective leaders stand out from the crowd. They have the ability to manage their state; being conscious of how they are feeling and managing those feelings and behaviour so as not to negatively impact on a given situation, as well as being aware of how situations affect them as individuals. This subsequently allows them to manage themselves prior to and during situations or events occurring. It also allows for the development of a deeper sense of emotional intelligence, which supports a more extensive appreciation of how those around them are affected by challenging situations that may stimulate an emotional response.

Self-awareness promotes the ability to remain level headed and considered, partly because there is an understanding that the situation, such as it is, should not be regarded as personal. It is important to remain professional in your interpretation, especially when things are going wrong and the people around you seem to be either losing control or finding it difficult to make sense of a rapidly unfolding situation or series of events. Self-awareness promotes calmness and stability, allowing you to employ critical thinking and logic; useful tools in circumstances such as these. The ability to apply them is a skill in itself and is something that will not go unnoticed by your team who will look to you for guidance, support and comfort. A failure to demonstrate that you can manage yourself in circumstances such as these may unsettle them, cause them to doubt you and your ability, which could potentially lead to an open or covert challenge/s to your leadership.

Self-awareness, like any other skill, can be developed and improved over time, through practice or the use of a competent coach or mentor.

The process of development often begins with the appreciation that many emotional and behavioural responses are learned, and as such can be altered, if you allow yourself to see the situation for what it is, as opposed to what you think it may be.

This is achieved through questioning and assessing the responses you provide to any given situation. If you simply allow yourself to become upset, you are less likely to be dealing with the issue at hand and are more likely to be responding to it. There are techniques you can employ to help maintain your focus: '7/11 breathing', a technique of breathing steadily and slowly, in through the nose – counting from one to seven on each in breath, then counting at the same rate, count from one to eleven on each out breath. This is a way of altering the initial perception of the situation or event as being a stressful one, where you question your own ability to cope with what is happening. You instead alter this perception and, as a result of slowing things down, allow yourself to regard it as a more solvable problem. This technique is often used as a component in stress and anger management. 'Anchoring', a technique used in Neuro Linguistic Programming (NLP) can also assist in the management of negative feelings and or emotions. Once you are in a position to manage your state, you are far more likely to manage the situation in a systematic, logical and intelligent manner. The ability to apply critical thinking will also assist in maintaining a solution-focused approach.

BEING A VISIBLE AND APPROACHABLE LEADER

Effective leaders are both visible and approachable. Your colleagues should know who you are, which includes knowing your name and your role. Simply being able to point you out in a crowd is not enough!

Showing up once a year for a team meeting and then leaving your staff/colleagues, management and supervisors to their own devices in the meantime may have a negative effect on them, unless you have taken the time and effort to reinforce your vision, outcome/s and expectations of them based on the organisational values through conscious and effective development and assessment of your team along the 'leadership continuum' (fig 1.2). If not, you may find that such an approach provides little or no direction and as a result fails to develop a sense of commitment, belonging or loyalty to you and or the organisation. Your people may lose focus and begin to operate in a leadership vacuum, with little or no idea what is expected of them as individuals or as members of the team/organisation. This level of detachment is where emphasis, vision and integrity are lost. It can increase the likelihood of your staff/colleagues developing an 'every person for themselves' approach to their work, meaning your once highly motivated and well-intentioned people become a group of individuals performing tasks with little or no real idea/interest in your desired outcome (see: case study two, Appendix 'A').

Being approachable is a fundamental requirement of effective leadership. Successful leaders do not shy away from their team. They will take time to listen to what they have to say, perhaps share a cup of tea or coffee from time to time, visiting out of the way locations at which their teams work to ensure that the people who work there know that they have not forgotten about them and continue to value their input. Effective leaders will encourage their colleagues to use their first name, in an attempt to remove antiquated principles of hierarchy, thus communicating that they are not unlike everyone else, they merely have a different job. They will keep their ear to the ground allowing them to be apprised of new and innovative ideas/approaches that could potentially make a difference to practices and processes within their teams and or the organisation. An effective leader will not only use this approach to actively develop and inspire their personnel, but also to maintain his/her capacity to establish links between individuals, groups, sections or departments in order to promote change and stimulate development.

TAKING RESPONSIBILITY

For some leaders the idea of taking responsibility for their team is akin to professional suicide. However, for the effective leader, taking responsibility is an obvious choice.

Taking responsibility for your team demonstrates that you are someone who can and will take charge of a situation. The leader with the willingness and ability to do this sends a very clear message to their team. "I am responsible for you, I am responsible for me; I am responsible to the organisation."

This type of leader has the attention and respect of those who work for and with him/her, as well as the respect and attention of those to whom they are responsible. This leader is far more likely to be trusted by his/her team, and the team is more likely to work well, as much for the leader as the organisation. Being able to harness this enthusiasm will assist you in establishing a well-focused and highly productive team capable of understanding and delivering your vision in-line with organisational values.

Address issues as they arise, don't let them fester!

As a leader a part of taking responsibility is addressing issues as they arise and not allowing them to fester. There are a number of potentially effective leaders that allow themselves to fall at this very important hurdle. Your level of involvement here will be dependent upon your position along the leadership continuum: fig 1.2. If, for example, one of your colleagues or a member of your staff has made some form of inappropriate comment/s, demonstrated some less than desirable behaviour or practice/s it is your responsibility or that of your supervisor or manager to bring this to the individual's attention at the earliest opportunity. Leaving the situation, perhaps because you are hoping that it will go away, will right itself or that the person concerned will realise what they have done and simply never do it again, is avoiding the situation and is not the way to go.

Failing to tackle issues in a timely manner can cause situations to fester unnecessarily. Believing that the person in question must have known that what they did was wrong is not the way to lead a team. Admittedly the situation or issue may be obvious to you but this does not mean that it is obvious to everyone or even anyone, else. The fact is that the person/s concerned may genuinely have no idea that they have done something wrong, and if in your defence you retort: "Well you should have known", then you have strayed into dangerous territory because the simple fact is: 'You don't know what you don't know'. As we have already discussed, as a leader it is your responsibility to regularly assess the extent of the your team/s or organisation's knowledge, either personally or via your supervisory/managerial staff, filling in the gaps wherever possible, through training, advice and guidance, coaching etc. So the sooner you address whatever issues you see arising, including any you may have inherited, the less likely you are to find yourself caught up in a chain of potentially unfortunate, unproductive and avoidable events.

POLICY, GOOD PRACTICE AND STANDARD OPERATING PROCEDURE

Do you have them?
Do you implement them?

In almost every organisation, whether in the public or private sector, you will find a range of policies, standard operating procedures and good practice statements. More often than not it is the job of the leaders and or management to ensure that these means of direction and guidance are adhered to. That being said, a large number of organisations have policies, procedural guidelines and practices that are not being followed on a day-to-day basis by the people on the ground. This may be due to the fact that some employees have no idea that they even exist. Others may know that they exist but have little idea of exactly what they contain and or mean, unless of course they are required to know as a result of some managerial scrutiny or assessment process.

As an effective leader (know exactly what is expected of you), it is your business to establish what the current policies, good practice statements and standard operating procedures (S.O.P.)

actually are in your area of business, and to establish whether or not they are actually being followed by your general, supervisory and managerial staff, as applicable. The absence of a structured and collective approach towards achieving awareness and implementation of established policy, procedure and accepted good practice could leave you, your team and your organisation increasingly exposed to the suggestion of impropriety, misconduct and potentially litigation.

An effective leader appreciates the fact that policies, procedures and good practice have been identified for a reason, often because it is believed that employing these tools will lead to a more stable, productive and efficient working environment resulting in the continued success of that organisation. To that end, an effective leader makes it their business to ensure that, not only are their staff/colleagues aware of current policies and procedure, but any literature relating to the same is easily accessible (not locked away in a filing cabinet etc) by you and your staff/colleagues and is presented in a format that is both legible and easily understood. Take it upon yourself to provide training where required and seek to clarify with your colleagues/ staff, why this level of awareness and implementation is important. Direct links should be made to organisational values, your vision for the team, its resilience and the future of the team within the organisation.

It is also important to appreciate that, as an effective leader, you should have a good working knowledge of the policies, procedure/s and good practice that exist within the organisation, and in particular those which relate to your area of business.

WE MAY BE BETTER THAN THOSE AROUND US, BUT ARE WE THE BEST WE CAN BE?

There are some individuals or teams who have been identified as the best in their field, category or group, which is an achievement in itself, especially when this accolade has been bestowed upon them by their peers. The question is however, are you the best that you can be?

There may be a sense that once such an accolade has been achieved, it is an acknowledgement that the group has done all it needs to and that collectively you have reached the proverbial mountaintop. In reality, however, although such an accolade can and should be regarded as an achievement in itself, there is still always more to do.

Being the best is about much more than reaching your outcome or being praised by those around you; it is about understanding what practices, processes and values assisted you in achieving that position in the first place; it is about appreciating that once you have achieved the desired outcome, maintaining your success requires ongoing action. The continuous reflection and review of practices, processes and values, along with your ability to rise to internal and external challenges consistently, are what will increase the likelihood of you and your team staying ahead of everyone else. Robust and continuous reflection, adjustment, implementation, training and development are required. An effective leader not only recognises this, s/he embraces it and makes it an integral part of their day-to-day practice. This is hard work and in many ways a leader may find it just as challenging, if not more so, as getting to this position in the first place.

The practices outlined in this book are not merely a stepping-stone to success; the process is more fundamental than that. The principles outlined here address the beginning, middle and continued progression of effective leadership. As previously stated in this book, the 'conscious competence' model explains the process and stages of learning a new skill. The origins of this model are unclear and it is often attributed to either Noel Burch or Abraham Maslow. Either way, the final stage of this four-stage model is regarded as the ultimate in the clarity and awareness of learning; unconscious competence: the point at which the learner becomes unconsciously competent in a task or ability. The Phoenix Leadership Programme does not subscribe to the notion that the four-stage theory is complete, and suggests that there is a fifth-stage of development: Reflective Competence In Action (fig 1.3): this stage of development suggests that once the learner has achieved unconscious competence, s/he has the ability to acquire a deeper level of knowledge and ability, through conscious and competent reflection, on their own and on other people's abilities and performance. This enables them to teach and coach others, while being actively aware of their own need to develop, maintain or acquire skills in new or existing areas.

Reflective Competence In Action; its implementation and the development of yourself and others in conjunction with the leadership continuum (fig 1.2) is a highly rewarding state, one that the Phoenix Leadership Programme can help you to achieve, and maintain.

CREATING THE MOOD FOR DEVELOPMENT

One of the things you will have read throughout this book is the need for you, the leader, to establish what your outcome is. It is important to know what you want to achieve, and, where possible, communicate the outcome to your team by including them in the process. Some organisations have a "need to know" policy and in agencies such as these the ability to share information regarding strategic or operational procedure or direction is understandably restricted.

There are three considerations an effective leader needs to contemplate in order to increase the probability of achieving a positive outcome:

'Personal': On a personal level, what elements of your personality will you need to call upon or play down in order to get the job done and how will that relate to your own concept of success?

'Strategic': Do you have the strategic capacity to undertake this task on your own or will you need the help of others? If so, can you identify those who can and will assist you in achieving your outcome?

'Organisational': Are the values and requirements of the organisation well served by what you intend to do and how you intend to do it?

If you can answer these questions positively then arguably you are on the right track. If, however, you are having difficulty or are under the impression that the answers to these questions are irrelevant, then it is likely that your actions have not been fully considered and may result in costly mistakes, delays or failure (see: case study one; appendix 'A').

Once your desired outcome has been established it is important to have an appreciation of how to create the right mood for change and development. Your colleagues may be apprehensive about change, many people are, but this is where you come in. Some leaders talk about how beneficial change will be and how everything may be a little hectic during the change process but suggest that things will be much more manageable and practical once the implementation phase is reached. It is rare that your colleagues will be naïve enough to believe that change is either a quick or painless process. Be honest with them because if you are not, it won't take them long to realise that they have been misled. This can create resentment, mistrust and as a result your colleagues are less likely to be supportive of you and the process of change, making your job harder than it needs to be. Creating the right mood for development/change is about knowing what your colleagues want, getting them excited about contributing to something new, giving them ownership of something they can be an integral part of and valuing their contribution as individuals, members of a team and ultimately, as members of the organisation; an organisation that takes them, their thoughts and their suggestions seriously.

Valuing members of your team is both powerful and empowering; it can be as simple as verbally acknowledging their contribution to a task and thanking them for their efforts, presenting their ideas as their ideas, or encouraging and supporting them to do so, informing the group how well you believe they work as a team and thanking them for their continued hard work, or providing some kind of monetary reward to the group or individual/s within the group who have performed particularly well. It is important to note however, that any monetary awards for individuals should be managed carefully so as not to foster resentment within the rest of the group/s. It is necessary to promote the strengths of your colleagues, while finding ways to overcome their weaknesses, thus nurturing increased confidence and capability. Ultimately, the goal of development should not be regarded or represented as solely focused on the financial profitability or other improvement of the organisation. Its aim should be to assist the continued development, growth and education of your staff/colleagues in the first instance. The knock on effect of this is that the organisation benefits from a more confident, better equipped and more skilled workforce. Where this is not the case, employees may feel like nameless cogs in an unfeeling machine, which may also affect their efficacy and commitment to the organisation and what it hopes to achieve.

The Boomerang Theory of Leadership

This theory relates to you temporarily transferring an aspect of your leadership role to a member of your team and allowing them take the lead. It may be part of an agreed action plan or period of development. You may have identified the fact that a specific individual has more experience than you in a particular field or area and decide to take full advantage of their knowledge and experience by allowing them to lead. Either way, you need to take a step back, provide support from the sidelines (be visible, not intrusive) as and when required and let your colleague(s) take control of the task or project for the interim. On completion, conduct a one-to-one assessment of their period in charge. Ask them how the process was for them. Encourage them to share their personal insight into their performance and offer your feedback on how you think the process went.

Once you are comfortable with this concept, you will find that its application can be effective in wide a range of situations, addressing such things as: staff development, conflict resolution and team building (*the boomerang theory is a prime example of the leadership continuum in action, fig 1.2*).

KEEPING YOUR PROFESSIONAL DISTANCE

Some leaders try to positively influence their relationships with their staff/colleagues by becoming their friends, going out for drinks on a regular or semi regular basis, and or sharing personal or intimate details of their lives. This approach can have its advantages as well as its disadvantages. If this is your approach be careful; your colleagues are not your friends, you are there to inform, lead, support and challenge them, something which is much more difficult to do under the banner of friendship. The author is not suggesting that as a leader you should not be friendly, or that there aren't leaders who have managed to do this successfully. Instead, what is being said is that there is an undeniable difference between friendship and leadership and in order to maintain an objective professional relationship it is prudent to allow your friendships and your position of leader to remain mutually exclusive.

Why?

Confronting and managing difficult performance issues such as your supervisors' and managers', inappropriate language, behaviour, tardiness and unprofessionalism are much more difficult when you are tackling such issues with a friend rather than a member of staff. Their perception of you is more likely to be objective and professional if they see you as their leader, the same will be true of their relationships with their staff/colleagues, and as a result, they are less likely to regard the challenge as a personal attack. Some leaders argue that they have no problem with making the transition from friend to leader, manager or supervisor when at work and this may be true for you as an individual, but can the same be said for your staff/colleagues? The resulting response to such a challenge may be wholly inappropriate, especially if the exchange inadvertently takes place in the presence of other personnel. This has the potential to undermine you and your leadership, as well as creating a situation that now requires you to be seen to take definitive action.

Effective leaders maintain their professional distance and promote such behaviour through the leadership continuum (fig 1.2). They have no problems with interacting with their colleagues in formal or social settings: leaving do's, Christmas parties etc, but at the same time manage to observe an appropriate level of professionalism without developing friendships or becoming over familiar.

CREATING AN AUDIT TRAIL

The ability to remember everything you said, queried or authorised with every person you have ever spoken with during the course of your work, both inside and outside of your organisation is virtually impossible. The use of e-mail may not be the most personal way to communicate with people, but it does provide you with an effective audit trail that you can use to track what has been said, agreed or shared with the people you work with and for. It is much easier to evidence the exchange of opinions, views and instructions that took place between yourself and others, organised in easy to access folders on your computer or in your personal files. As with anything computer based, the backing up of information and documents is an absolute necessity.

However, that being said, and where possible you should avoid allowing e-mail to become your sole or main source of communication. It does not provide you with the valued face-to-face or verbal contact that an effective leader uses to reinforce their communication with others. E-mail is merely a tool to assist communication and should be viewed as such. Creating an audit trail also serves a strategic function, especially when dealing with individuals who make rash, costly and ineffective suggestions or decisions. Asking for or sharing information regarding any issues via e-mail provides you with some insurance when questions are asked regarding who said what and who authorised what and when. It can help to avoid the tiresome "he said", "she said" scenario and provide hard evidence of what transpired, which would also include any questions you have asked, the subsequent answers and any instructions you received or gave. A skilled operator will read an e-mail and make a point of telephoning or coming to see you in order to provide a verbal response, in which case you should take it upon yourself to send a further e-mail detailing the verbal exchange, asking the person/s in question to confirm what had been agreed or decided verbally. If at any time you are of the opinion that these e-mails may be used to defend or fortify your position or that of your team or organisation, be mindful to request delivery and read receipts.

IT IS YOU THAT HAS CHANGED, NOT THOSE AROUND YOU

Undertaking the Phoenix Leadership Programme will yield some noticeable and very positive results. One thing to remember is that the process is about you, the way in which you manage yourself, the way you influence those around you as well as how you promote development and cohesion among your personnel. This process is highly impactive and will become second nature with practice, leading to your ability to achieve reflective competence in action (fig 1.3). You will also become increasingly aware of how those around you, your peers, and your leaders interact with you.

Regardless of how you interpret what they do and how they do it, remember it is you who has changed, not them. Your newfound clarity is a result of your commitment to your continued development; you have worked hard to achieve it, be proud of yourself and remember, "Once you have achieved your goal, it is the start of a new beginning."

APPENDIX
CASE STUDIES

Case Study One:

Paul and his team of eight were tasked with travelling to Spain in order to collect some precious cargo from their Spanish counterparts. He was given instructions to obtain a detailed briefing on the cargo, including transportation, ensure the safe delivery of said cargo to the UK and upon its arrival, onward transfer to the new owners. Paul and his team had undertaken similar projects, albeit only within the UK, and as a result he did not foresee any difficulties; however, it soon became apparent that there were a number of differences with this assignment.

Firstly, Paul had volunteered to lead a team of highly experienced people; many of who possessed the skills to perform the role of team leader. In addition, this project involved new territory for Paul and his team; they were travelling to a different country and Paul had not factored in how the team would behave abroad nor considered whether he would have to adapt his leadership style to accommodate the changes in their environment. Upon arriving in Spain and meeting with their Spanish colleagues, arrangements were made to meet up again the following day. The next morning Paul decided not to have a formal team meeting, and therefore did not discuss the desired outcomes and objectives with the team, neither prior to, nor after their arrival in Spain.

The meeting he had planned with his Spanish colleagues to discuss the detailed logistics of the project lasted until lunchtime, after which time he and his team returned to their hotel and enjoyed some time to themselves. That evening they met up and their conversations were centered on going out and 'having a good time' rather than discussing the details of the project at hand. Concerned by the general lack of interest in the job they were there to do, Paul felt that he was losing control of the group, he knew that he needed to re-evaluate his approach in order to get himself and his team back on track.

There are number of identifiable issues regarding this situation:

By not establishing and sharing his overall outcome and objectives with his team, his leadership was affectively absent, and the team did not understand that it was important that their behaviour reflected the organisational values, while they were working abroad. Paul had allowed them to set their own agenda, which consisted of having a good time while they were away. Getting the job done in a professional manner was a secondary consideration; they believed they could simply call upon their previous experience/s in order to complete the task in hand. Paul had also neglected to evaluate his 'Personal', 'Strategic' and 'Organisational' considerations:

'Personal': On a personal level, what elements of your personality will you need to call upon or play down in order to get the job done and how will that relate to your own concept of success?

'Strategic': Do you have the strategic capacity to undertake this task on your own or will you need the help of others? If so, can you identify those who can and will assist you in achieving your outcome?

'Organisational': Are the values and requirements of the organisation well served by what you intend to do and how you intend to do it?

This process would have helped Paul to appreciate the importance of establishing a clear line of communication with his team regarding their role and his expectations of them ('Personal'), 'Strategic'- Paul's capacity to undertake this task could have been bolstered by enlisting the assistance of one or more of the senior and well-established members of the team to help and support him in achieving his outcome. Getting buy-in from them at the earliest opportunity would have reinforced his position as the team leader and allowed him articulate the level of professionalism he expected from them, both as individuals and as a group. 'Organisational'- in applying these elements from the outset, Paul would have been able to achieve his outcome in such a way that the organisational values and requirements would have been met.

Options and Consequences:

Paul had three options; firstly: he could have done nothing, and allowed his team to have a night out drinking, accepting the possibility that they may or may not get themselves into trouble. Once the team had "got it out of their system", his staff would be able to focus on the task at hand and begin to demonstrate the level of skill and professionalism they had shown on previous jobs.

Secondly, Paul could have pulled rank, reminded his team that he was in charge, and demanded that they follow his instructions and to forget about going drinking and insisted that they focus their attentions on the job they were there to do.

The third option was that Paul could have addressed the issue with his team, in an attempt to rectify the situation, and in doing so; increase the likelihood of him and his team achieving a successful outcome.

Which one would you choose, and why?

Consequences:

Each one of the aforementioned options has consequences. If Paul chose to do nothing, he would be placing both himself, and his team in a vulnerable position, because he would have passed up the opportunity to get his team back on track, and in doing so, he would have compromised the potential of completing the job successfully.

Secondly; Paul could have pulled rank and demanded that his team follow his instructions; it is certainly one-way to get things done. However, the consequences of taking such a stance may be that you cause your staff/colleagues to act under duress. You will probably get exactly what you ask for and nothing more. It is not an approach that inspires confidence in you, nor is it one that creates buy-in from your team. It can also create tension, disharmony and resentment towards you, and as a result, it is unlikely that you will get the best out of your team.

Addressing the issues with his staff /colleagues also has consequences. Paul's team may not have responded well to what they were being asked to do, they may also have disagreed with his assessment of the situation and informed him of that fact. His challenge could have ended in confrontation. On the other hand, it may have helped his colleagues to recognise that their behaviour did not reflect the company values and, as such, was not compatible with how the organisation expected or wanted things to be done.

If we refer to the Leadership Cycle: the five-stage model identifies how actual development and effectiveness is achieved, reviewed and maintained (fig 1.1), we can see that Paul was able to identify a problem. He recognised that his team had not fully understood why this task needed to be addressed in the way that reflected the organisational values. This lack of understanding identified that the Leadership Cycle was incomplete, and if it remained incomplete, it was unlikely that Paul and his team would have been able to achieve their outcome. It is apparent that Paul needed to take some form of definitive action in order to adequately resolve the situation.

Paul took some time out and re-evaluated his approach in line with the principles of the Phoenix Leadership Programme. He concluded that on a 'personal' level he needed to better utilise his skills as a communicator, along with his personal knowledge of this group, to inform them of his intended outcome and the part they had to play in achieving it. With regards to the Leadership Cycle, Paul needed to know that his team understood why it was important for them to behave in accordance with the organisational values while undertaking their first international job. 'Strategically' he would need to assign specific tasks to the more senior and well-established members of the group, knowing that once they were tasked, in this case with overall discipline and professionalism of the group, alongside himself; their authority would not be questioned (such was the nature of the group). Finally, although it may seem to some that the management of the group's extra curricular activity may be a little over the top, Paul knew that any incident of drunkenness, a lack of professional courtesy etc reported to their employers, would reflect negatively upon him, the group and the organisation. Consequently he knew that the organisation would be well served by what he intended to do and how he intended to do it. In fact Paul implemented this course of action and found it to be very successful. Upon their return to the UK, his employers commended him and his team for their professionalism and overall success in transporting the cargo to the UK intact and without incident.

Case Study Two:

Sarah was the manager of a small team of outreach officers responsible for establishing and maintaining contact with internal and external stakeholders in the field of community service, where she strived to be a successful leader.

She believed the best way to achieve this was by having the best team she could assemble and, in some cases, actively head hunted new members of staff.

Sarah knew that her organisation valued knowledge and was therefore determined to accrue as much knowledge as she could around her area of expertise. As a result, she spent a large proportion of her time writing reports on policy and procedure for a range of different departments within the organisation.

She became known for her ability to produce policy documents within a matter of days, which in turn led to an increase in requests for assistance in writing various policies.

This additional demand resulted in her having less time to provide her team with the direction they needed to achieve their aims and objectives and a lack of clarity in how they should go about doing this. Sarah believed that her choice of staff, i.e. people who could work on their own initiative and without close supervision, would allow her the time she needed to concentrate on her own work. She considered the latter more important in making sure senior leaders would notice her.

During this time Sarah's team were performing well, they were able to work efficiently, attended the relevant meetings, responded to requests from senior managers and provided a comprehensive service to the organisation as a whole.

On the occasions when Sarah did attend meetings she became aware that her team had developed a considerable knowledge base, were able to answer complex questions and had become skilled in presenting the information requested.

Consequently, Sarah started to feel 'out of the loop' so she would quite often attempt to add her own opinions to those of her staff; thoughts that often contradicted their answers and suggestions.

Unaware of her behaviour and the impact it was having, Sarah continued to interact in this manner until one meeting, attended by two senior directors, Sarah became embroiled in a confrontational situation with a member of her team (Andy), something duly noted by the directors present, both of whom became physically uncomfortable with the sudden turn of events.

After the meeting, perplexed by what had occurred, Sarah had a conversation with Andy and asked what had caused him to behave in such a manner. Andy informed her that she had spoken to him as if he were incompetent and went on to explain that this was something she had done to him previously, along with other members of her staff, and it was becoming a regular occurrence.

Shocked by Andy's revelation, Sarah advised him that her behaviour had not been intentional, to which Andy suggested that if this was genuinely the case, she needed to consider why her staff were increasingly unhappy with the way she spoke to them, especially during meetings.

Andy added that the team viewed Sarah as someone who wanted to keep all of the knowledge to herself and for them to have nothing, despite the fact that they were dealing with complex work issues on a day-to-day basis and had developed notable skills and abilities in their area.

Sarah came away from the meeting confused and concerned.

After a detailed discussion and an honest assessment of her recent leadership/ managerial performance, it became apparent to Sarah that she had allowed herself to become detached from her staff and in doing so had ceased to be the 'visible and approachable leader' she once was. Despite the fact that she had effectively left her staff to their own devices, Sarah wanted to appear as though she was still very much involved.

Sarah had not established a vision of how her team should work, either with her, or in her absence and was therefore unable to promote a clear and unambiguous way of working. Her approach provided little or no direction and as a result failed to stimulate a sense of commitment, belonging or loyalty to her on the part of the team. Rather, they were operating in a leadership vacuum with little or no idea what she expected of them, although, due to their own initiative, professionalism and awareness of the values that govern the strategic direction of the company, they were able to perform effectively, providing a quality service to the organisation.

There was another issue. Andy's response to Sarah in the meeting and his subsequent reference to how the team felt towards Sarah identified that her staff felt frustration toward her; something which she was able to address using elements of the Phoenix Conflict Resolution System (as mentioned earlier in the book).

Sarah knew that things had to change; she needed to become re-acquainted with her staff and considered how she could do this via the use of the Phoenix Leadership Programme. She concluded that 'Developing a sense of team' was what she needed to achieve, as well as diffusing any conflict that she had encountered, initially with Andy and potentially with the rest of the team.

Sarah saw that her staff were already producing some good work and had built up a wealth of knowledge in their area of business. She needed to identify what her outcome was, share that outcome with them, demonstrate that she regarded them as being capable and worthy of working alongside her and that she wanted to work alongside them. Sarah began to facilitate team meetings with specific agenda items, allowing members of her team to deliver those agenda items, thus creating a space where her team could identify and share their areas of expertise, enabling her and their colleagues to learn from them in the process. She took time to value those contributions and suggested ways in which they may benefit the team and the organisation alike. Sarah followed this up by discussing the suggestions made by those concerned in their monthly one-to-one meetings, encouraging her staff to lead on the discussion about their idea/s, possible implementation (where applicable) and any subsequent results or anticipated outcomes.

The approach worked well and, within several months, Sarah had managed to demonstrate a new way of working with her staff. They became more inclined to share their thoughts and a range of ideas, not just with each other but also with Sarah. She became an integral part of the process and her team started to look to her for leadership and clarity. Her new approach also addressed the issue of frustration and conflict that Andy had identified previously. Sarah's approach included the use 'Reflective Competence in Action' (fig1.3). She made herself aware of how she communicated with her staff/colleagues, being mindful of what she was trying to achieve and how they were responding to her desired outcome, as well as how she must respond in order to achieve the most satisfactory outcome possible; while considering how their own level of competence, 'conscious or otherwise', may be affecting the interaction. Sarah found that although she became busier with her team, she was able to successfully manage her time between her team, its continued development and success and her policy writing.

Case Study Three:

Lisa, a sergeant, qualified police trainer and trainer of trainers, had been tasked with overseeing the training and development of five new members of staff, who had recently completed their trainer's qualification and all of whom were new to the field of training.

Being an experienced and competent trainer, Lisa was aware that she would need to spend a large portion of her time supporting the development of her new staff.

Lisa was aware of the Phoenix Leadership Programme and opted to use the 'Leadership Continuum' (fig 1.2) to assist her in this role.

Using the first three of the six leadership principles:

'Inform':

If you take over a new team/section, you should inform your personnel who you are, apprise them of your background, including any relevant experience or qualifications. It is important to inform your colleagues of your vision for the future, what you expect from them as individuals and as a team, identify the values that underpin what it is you will be doing and how you envisage that you/they will achieve it. It may be prudent to inform them of what the organisation requires of you as a leader as well as what they (your team) can expect from you.

'Lead':

You are likely to encounter some members of your team who are happy to accept your (new) vision and are ready to hit the ground running. They will be led by your example, demonstrate your ability to lead by doing just that, be the person who is first in and the last out. Show that you are someone who actively promotes the values of the organisation and their vision for the organisation through what they say and what they do on a day-to-day basis, it will encourage your team to do the same.

'Discuss':

You may find that some of your colleagues are not fully committed to your vision at first and will wait on the sidelines performing their duties as requested, though not yet convinced of your approach. You are just as likely to encounter those who are less enthusiastic and will take every opportunity to question your judgment and your vision, both in public and or in private. It is at times such as these that your ability to discuss opposing issues or concerns with the relevant member(s) of your team is very important. Effective leaders are keen to discuss issues that arise, making it their business to ensure that their vision is clear and their message is understood. An unwillingness or inability to do this can lead to a breakdown in communication, which in turn may lead to a loss of respect for that leader, the knock-on effect being that when a team loses faith in you, you will likely lose faith in and respect for them and their collective ability as a team.

Lisa met with her new trainers and asked them to consider what they felt their current strengths and areas of development were as trainers. Their responses allowed her to establish an initial 'flexible' outcome for each of the trainers, i.e. she began to consider how best to support her colleagues; building their confidence and develop their skills and abilities as trainers.

Lisa followed this up with visual assessments of each of the trainers at work, checking to see if their evaluations of their strengths and areas of development mapped across to how they performed in practice. Lisa identified that her novice trainers were quite accurate in assessing their own training abilities and she was able to establish a programme of development utilising the 'Leadership Continuum'. Over a period of several months Lisa was able to support and gauge the progress of her trainers, assisting them to move from the position of 'novice' along the 'development phase', increasing their confidence and ability through achievement, and latterly into 'leader' (in their own right), where the trainers where able to conduct their own training classes with minimum input/direction from Lisa.

The 'Leadership Continuum' proved to be instrumental in providing Lisa with a vehicle to begin the overall and systematic development of her training staff.

INDEX

REVIEWS

"I wish this book could come to life and talk to me; it's like having a pocket sized mentor to guide and inspire you. I've become a Leader and a more effective Manager all in one".

Government Manager, Salford.

"An informative and truly refreshing read, cuts through the difficult 'management-speak', presenting key concepts and ideas in a straightforward and easy to follow way. Highly recommended".

Senior Public Sector Manager, Manchester.

"I've done many management courses and read innumerable books about management over the years and come away from them without improving anything I do. What I love about the Phoenix approach is that it doesn't let you off the hook - it helps you learn the knowledge and understand it, then importantly takes you beyond that to developing that knowledge into new skills".

Steve; (Police Sergeant) Manager,
Performance & Quality Assurance.

www.ingramcontent.com/pod-product-compliance
Ingram Content Group UK Ltd.
Pitfield, Milton Keynes, MK11 3LW, UK
UKHW020139250726
13967UKWH00002B/744

9 781491 274064